D0710109

THE CORN MOTHER

Published by: A Year In The Country, 2020
All rights reserved. No part of this publication may be
reproduced or transmitted in any form or by any means
(electronic, mechanical, photocopying, recording or
otherwise) without permissions from the publishers.
www.ayearinthecountry.co.uk

ISBN: 978-1-9160952-1-2

Copyright © Stephen Prince, 2020
The right of Stephen Prince to be identified as the author
of this work has been asserted by him in accordance with
the Copyright, Designs & Patent Act 1988.

This book is a work of fiction. Except in the case of
historical fact, any resemblance to actual persons,
living or dead, is purely coincidental.

Design and cover image: Stephen Prince /A Year In The Country
The layout is based in part on design work by Ian Lowey of
Bopcap Book Services, Manchester.

Other books by Stephen Prince:
A Year In The Country: Wandering Through Spectral Fields
A Year In The Country: Straying From The Pathways
A Year In The Country: The Marks Upon The Land

Albums by Stephen Prince:
The Corn Mother: Night Wraiths

Albums by Stephen Prince (working as A Year In The Country):
Airwaves: Songs From The Sentinels
No More Unto The Dance
Undercurrents

THE CORN MOTHER

Stephen Prince

1/4

1877: Ms Jessop

I've lived here all my life. It's the only place I know. Some folk from round here talk about going to live elsewhere, of jobs in the city but that's not for me. I like to watch the cycles of life and the year. To cook my own food that I've helped to pluck from the ground and water that I've carried in from the well.

It's a hard life and not for everybody but its the one for me. Even when the crops failed I wouldn't have left. Where would I go? To a stinking hovel in the city and spend my days chained by the factory clock to a weaving machine? No. Not for this lass.

But it can be difficult knowing everybody and everybody knowing you and your business. From time to time I wake in the middle of the night and I just wander the fields. It gives me space to think. To just be. I can still hear the animals in the woods but it's peaceful, away from those infernal steam engines that they've started to use for the ploughing and to carry feed and produce. They say its progress but I'm not so sure.

1878: John

She was out there again last night. Walking the fields on her own. She thinks nobody has seen her but I have.

What's she doing out there? You've got to let the land rest for the night if you want it to be bountiful. That's what my grandmother told me. She's not letting it rest, not letting it be.

I'm going to have to tell somebody. Maybe me mam, maybe Mr Smithwick. Something's got to be done.

1878: Mr Smithwick

Young John's mother told me about what he'd seen. Ms Jessop walking the fields alone at night. I told his mother not to tell anybody else but it was too late, she already had, and you can no more stop the passage of that kind of gossip through this village than cause the wind to pause in the fields or the rain to stay in the clouds.

I've called a meeting with the others to discuss the matter. First though I'll go and have a quiet talk with Ms Jessop, tell her to stay indoors at night like all the other good folk.

1878: Mr Smithwick

That's just what we need. That old tittle-tattle Mrs Worthword has been gossiping and saying that Ms Jessop has been wandering the fields at night so that she can curse the crops. That she practises witchcraft and was responsible for the crops failing last decade, when anybody with common sense knows it was a natural blight and too much wet weather that did for them.

The problem is that the villagers are scared. They remember that ruinous year all too well and they're worried it will come again. They're just ordinary, simple folk and they put far too much trust in folk tales.

Most of their families have lived and worked here for generations without things changing all that much but with the new steam engines they're worried that they'll lose their livelihoods and be forced to leave and live amongst the smokestacks in the city.

We need to nip this in the bud before it gets out of hand.

1878: Ms Jessop

They came last night with burning torches. I'd heard them coming and so I'd taken away to the woods but I watched them from amongst the trees. At their head was Mrs Worthwood, like an aged pied piper, and there was a grim set to their faces.

When they discovered I wasn't there they set to on my cottage, smashing and tearing, throwing things out into the fields. I couldn't watch and couldn't look away.

1878: Mrs Wothword

She wasn't there. Fled on her broomstick I told the others, gone to join the Devil in his fiery underworld.

I made sure they noticed signs of her kinship with Old Nick. That black cat of her's hissed when we came in, that had them on edge, and then there were her jars of herbs and tinctures. Many in that crowd had been to her over the years to seek help with maladies but that has soon been forgotten and I had them all thinking they were potions she used in her witchery.

I'll have this cottage for my own. She won't dare show her face here again.

1878: Jeremiah

When that black cat started hissing at us I knew it was true. She was in league with something otherworldly.

And then there were all those jars of who knows what that she must have used in her rituals.

And them books. A whole row of them. Full of evil scriptures no doubt.

I just couldn't stop myself. There was a fire burning in the hearth, with nobody to tend it. What more proof do you need than that to tell you of the wickedness in that cottage?

I used pages from one of the books as a taper, lighting it from the fire and began to burn down the witch's home. The bedding took easily and soon the flames were on the thatch of the roof and we stood back to watch the cottage burn.

1878: Mrs Worthword

That damn fool Jeremiah. Born with half a brain and lost the little he had in the tavern. He burnt that cottage down. A perfectly good cottage it was and with her out of the way I knew that I'd have been able to talk my way into taking over the tenancy. It had a good acreage of land at the back that I could've kept a few goats and some chickens on. Since my Joseph passed away times have been hard and I've barely had enough to keep body and soul together.

I could have seen out my days in that cottage rather than spending them living amongst my oldest's family and his wife. I never could stand her. Thinks she knows best but she knows nothing.

1878: Ms Jessop

It's been a week now that I've been living in the woods. I've managed to stay out of sight and nobody bothers me here.

I've been living on what I can forage and a few nighttime raids on people's barns and food stores. There's water to drink from the local brook and I've been lucky that the weather has held.

It's given me time to think, to ponder about what I do now and next. I'm an outcast from my home and that hurts. I know that I shouldn't lash out in anger and revenge but I feel that I still will.

An idea came to me this morning when I was foraging and I saw those mushrooms growing. I just need to plan carefully and choose my moment.

1878: Emily

Jeremiah has been acting mighty strange these last couple of days. He's always been a bit unpredictable when he's drank some ale but this is different. His eyes seem wild and staring and he's ranting and raving about how he shouldn't have done it, how she's visiting him in the night to torment him and fill him full of guilt.

He seems to mean Ms Jessop who lived in that cottage they went mob-handed to the other week and ended up burning down. They've not found her, although some of the menfolk tried looking. That's just fuelled the rumours that she's fled with the Devil or some such fanciful nonsense. I expect she just saw sense when she heard them coming and has thought better of returning to live amongst such folk as would so easily turn against her.

Hopefully things will settle down over the next week or so and he'll get back to normal.

1878: Tom

The harvesting is nearly done. It's been glorious weather and a bountiful year. Maybe there's something in what folk have been saying about how ridding the village of that Ms Jessop has brought us good fortune.

When we're down to the last row of the corn harvest we'll knock it to the ground and put the spirit of the corn mother back into the earth, ready for her to be awoken by next year's sun. And then there will be much merriment as we'll know our work is done. There'll be a feast this evening and plenty of laughter. I'm looking forward to it, as are the other lads and the women folk, it's thirsty work this harvesting and it right brings on your appetite.

1878: Ms Jessop

I waited until they were all in the fields bringing the harvest in. It's a job for everybody, even the young uns, and so I've got the run of the village hall to myself.

I've learnt a thing or two through my years of ministering to the folk of this village. Learnt which of nature's plants can heal, soothe a sore stomach or throat, ease a fevered brow, speed a wound's mending.

And I know which plants can bring on a fever of the mind. Some of the younger lads in the village have been known to go a-mushrooming when they're in season and they come back to the village giggling and all daft.

But it's not only mushrooms that can turn a man's mind. There are other plants with subtler and not always predictable effects, that can leave you with dreams full of feverish thoughts and paranoia. Have you wandering who's for you and who's against you, for sometimes days or more after.

I've been trying out some on that big daft oaf Jeremiah, mixing some in with his ale when he's out in the fields. It only takes a dash or two in a drink for the effect to take hold.

I survey the fine spread that's laid out for later. Ales, cakes, stews and more. I think I'll start with the stews; they'll hide the taste and texture the best.

1878: Mr Smithwick

Ever since the night of the harvest feast the village has seemed somehow unsettled. Lifelong friends meet warily or won't talk at all. There is suspicion all around and little work being done.

There is much talk of people being visited in their dreams by the corn mother, who seems to be some kind of supernatural embodiment of Ms Jessop. People say she arrives as a wraithlike figure and while they sleep she enacts her revenge, souring and spoiling milk and food, bringing illness to livestock, ruination to crops and causing savings to disappear into thin air as a form of reparations.

I'd put it all down to guilt and related paranoia for burning the cottage down but the veterinary does seem to have been called out a lot of late and there has seemed to be a fair degree of ailment amongst the village.

What's this now? Ashton and Fowler brawling with Jeremiah in the middle of the street. I'll have to go over and try and stop the young fools.

1878: Ashton

I told that Jeremiah it was all his hot-headed fault. Burning that woman's cottage down and now her spirit is back for revenge. Me, him and Fowler ended up brawling in the street. He's a big lad but uncoordinated and we soon had him down in the dirt.

She arrives you know, in the night. Visits me in my dreams. I awake with a dreadful fever of the mind and her face haunting me, her black wraith's shawl flowing in the wind behind her. The corn mother, the vengeful spirit of Ms Jessop. She is visiting us all, one by one. Bringing ill fortune and never letting us forget the village's guilt.

I've had six cows down with illness this last week, me and the wife have had dreadful gutrot and now the small amount of coinage we'd managed to put aside has just disappeared. She's cursed this village. Or maybe we have.

And I just don't know who to trust anymore. Friends I've known since childhood are scheming against me, I can tell. They're after my wife, my land, my cattle.

1878: Ms Jessop

I watched them after the feast. Some seemed more affected than others but I'd started a fracture amongst my once home and it was growing, spreading, splitting off into a myriad directions.

I've been working towards my plan. I'm going to leave and start afresh somewhere new. I'll need a little money to do that. So carefully, ever so carefully, I've taken a little here and there from homes when folk were out. I only took from those I saw at my cottage the night they burned it down. I know that doesn't make it right though.

The illness amongst the cattle, the spoilt food and the gutrot? I could try and claim more power than I have but that's just some bad luck, some common sicknesses that are spreading through the village and what with them all slacking from work and house-keeping they're leaving food out too long in this ripe end-of-summer heat.

1879: Mr Smithwick

Me and some of the older folk in the village have tried to calm things down. Tried everything we could think of. Reasoned with people. Berated other's foolishness. But all to no avail.

There's something rotten in this village and I know not what. All I can say is that it started after that mob went to Ms Jessop's cottage.

Another family moved away today, more who have had enough, who have become fearful of this place and the so-called visits of the corn mother.

I saw them with all they could carry on the back of a cart. They wouldn't even tell me where they were going. They're not the first and shall not be the last. What started as a trickle is becoming a flood.

1879: Ms Jessop

I'm standing in the middle of the village. Nothing stirs. There's no smoke from a stove, no animals being fed, no children playing, nor women gossiping. Nothing.

I'm not sure if this is what I meant to happen but my once home is now a ghost, just a shell. Every family has left. Some fleeing with little more than they had on their backs.

They say you will reap what you sow. I'm not sure who planted this bitter harvest. Me, Jeremiah and that mob, or whoever turned them against me, but we must now all live with its fruits.

I take one last look and then turn away. I head south towards the city. I never thought that would be where my life would lead me but with a few coins in my pocket hopefully I can plough some kind of future away from all this and my memories.

1970: Peter

I've got this script I've been working on. I'd been watching all those gothic horror films, vampires, country mansions and all that in the cinemas for years and one day I thought to myself "I could do that, write one of these films, how hard could it be?"

Well, writing it's the easy part. Well, sort of. It's the selling it, getting paid, getting it made that's difficult. I've made a few tentative steps in that direction but nothing in earnest yet. The script still needs a bit more work.

I'm not new to this writing lark though. I was one of the main writers on an underground magazine until not so long ago. It was a good gig. Until it wasn't. We thought we were going to change the world, that the future was peacock bright, full of love and psychedelia. There seems to have been a heavy toll for those dreams for some, a fair few, shall we say, casualties.

One of which was my bank balance. I hadn't been paid for months, still kept submitting my articles, beavering away for the cause and all that. Temporary cash flow problems was what they kept telling me, they were just waiting for X, Y and Z to pay them and then everything would be fine again.

It wasn't. I'll mark it up to experience I guess.

Since then it's been baked beans and the odd bit of cash in hand work here and there. It's not quite all mod cons where I live but my rent's fairly cheap, which makes things easier.

It's going pretty well actually. I had this idea of a rural village in the 19th century, where the villagers decide wrong-headedly that one of their own has cursed their crops and the descent of the village into its own form of guilt-ridden madness after they take matters into their own hands.

I'm trying to step aside from all the more hammy side of horror, make something a bit more real I guess. We'll see how it goes.

1972: Alain

I get sent so many scripts. The curse of having had a few films that managed to do well at the box office and were also a critical success. They were fashionable even for a while. It's been a while since those days but the cachet they leant me still lingers.

This one though caught my eye. *The Corn Mother*. There was something in it. Something I couldn't quite put my finger on.

There were no indications of where it was set, although I assume Peter, the writer, had Britain in mind. But for me it conjured an almost never-neverland, placeless village. Nominally it was a horror thriller but I could see glimmers of other potential in the writing, space to create something a little more leftfield, to sneak in something a bit dreamlike under the guise of genre trappings.

When I met up with Peter he seemed open to suggestions. We had a good discussion about it all and I came away feeling positive.

Of course it's all down to the money. It always is. Conrad's not so bad, he understands the need sometimes for a bit of space and freedom when you're making a film but Gines, that buffoon. What does he know? Made his money in manufacturing and now he's moved into film but he's still applying the same sort of assembly line mentality to filmmaking as he had in his factories.

Yes, I understand. There is a need for a certain discipline within film productions but when you're turning money into the spectres of a story and then hopefully back into money again, it's not quite as straightforward as a factory flowchart.

I don't think Gines really understands the film. He's just thinking of how many peasant wenches in corsets we can get on the poster to help sell it. I know sometimes you have to play the game but the bottom line is all he thinks about.

Well, let's see what happens. Maybe him and Conrad will balance one another out. It's happened before.

1972: Peter

This bloody script. I wish I'd never started it. I've been working on it for a couple of years or more now and I've got dozens of versions sat around in my room.

I've just come back from another meeting with a potential producer. Believe it or not I've got an agent, all official and everything. Just a friend of a friend that I bumped into at a party. He's been sending the script out for a while now and there's been some interest, which is good, but nothing definite, which isn't.

Part of the problem is that everybody I have a meeting with seems to have their own ideas about the script, suggestions of how to make it better. Well, not so much suggestions, more "Change it like this and we'll think about making it". Only think about it mind.

For a while I really thought it was going to get the green light. This European director was interested. I've seen some of his stuff, it's pretty good. Quite highbrow in a continental kind of a way, i.e. still a bit smutty but wrapped up in arthouse stylings, so it's okay to like it. Actually, that sounds dismissive of his work, which I don't mean to be. When I met him I got the sense that he was a wily old fox. He didn't say anything but he seemed to understand the game, knew that if he added a certain amount of sauce to his films that it would make it easier to get them funded and to get the punters in once it was made. He was a realist in a way, he just hid it well.

But then the money disappeared. I don't know if the producers just decided it wasn't for them, couldn't see the market for it or what it was. The director seemed genuinely quite sorry about it, he took me out for something to eat and said he wished that he could make the film but it just wasn't to be.

1974: Peter

All these hours and years of working on the script and what happens?

I went to the pictures the other night to see this film *The Wicker Man* that had just opened. Really I just wanted a break from all the talk of the General Election and I'm sick of the electric going out at night 'cause of all the power shortages, what with the miners' disputes and trouble in the Middle East. They've introduced a three-day working week to save on fuel and half the time if you go to the pub you're having to drink by candle light.

I didn't know all that much about the film, I just wanted an escape for a couple of hours.

That's not quite what I got. This film, it had everything I've been aiming for with *The Corn Mother*. And more. It's sort of... well, indefinable really. Part horror, part detective thriller. Almost a musical. It's set rurally. There's a crop failure. People who live in a small community take matters into their own hands.

I was a bit knocked for six. At first I couldn't see how we'd ever get somebody to make *The Corn Mother* now. It's very different but there are enough similarities to scupper it.

Mind you, my agent says if *The Wicker Man* does well then that might help as producers might think that what worked once could work again.

1979: Peter

That's it. I'm done. No more. No more promises. No more getting my hopes up.

I've been offered a writing job. On one of the dailies. It's just grind work but it pays okay and what with Mary expecting I'm going to take it. I want to if I'm being honest. This living on dreams isn't working for me any more. It hasn't been for a while if truth be told.

I'm just going to put the script away. Let *The Corn Mother* sleep for a while, maybe for good. I gave it a good shot. We all did but it just doesn't seem like it's going to happen.

There's this one version that I really like. Not sure if anybody else ever did, apart from maybe that director Alain. It's quietly unsettling rather than being all brash and upfront. You're never quite sure what the villagers did and it's not so overly straightforward. It's more a portrait of the psyche of a community fracturing under its own dysfunction and the pressures brought to bear on it by internal and external conflicts.

I guess it's in part a reflection of what's been going on in Britain for much of this decade. Electricity blackouts and the Three-Day Week a few years or so ago and now we've had a load more strikes and general argy bargy this winter. It's been darned cold as well, which probably doesn't help. The Summer of Love seems like a long time ago now. Time to grow up a bit I guess.

Some people are talking about how this new government is the start of a clean sweep, a fresh start for the country. I don't know. I don't trust them. There's something about that Thatcher, something in her eyes. It's hard to properly trust somebody who took milk away from children.

In the meantime life goes on. I'm going to phone up the red top this afternoon and tell them yes. I'm kind of looking forward to it I think. Being part of society's machine, a semi-willing cog. I might even enjoy it.

1981: Sarah

I've been called in for an audition. About time to. Work's been pretty thin on the ground for the last few months. Well, actually, the last few years more like.

The film's script seems to have been knocking around for a while now. Somebody else I knew, I think, auditioned for it in the seventies. Nothing came of it. I don't know if anything will now. You can but try.

When they sent me the script I got two for some reason, they arrived separately and they're both quite different. I'm not sure which one I'm meant to have read or be testing for. I phoned my agent to ask her if she could find out which was the right one. She phoned me back and said nobody at the production company's office seemed to know, so I'll just have to wing it a bit I guess.

I'm up for the part of Ms Jessop. It's sort of the lead. I say that because although she features pretty heavily near the start of the film, she disappears part of the way through, possibly chased out of her village by other locals who think she's cursed their crops. In one of scripts she comes back as a form of night monster who terrorises the villagers that persecuted her. In the other one though... well, it's hard to quite fathom what happens. She's reappears, or at least her spirit or phantom does, or maybe it's just that the villagers think she has and their guilt drives them mad.

Anyways, time to get ready; I've got a taxi booked for three o'clock. Best try and make myself presentable, smarten up a bit, put on a good front and all that. Wish me luck.

1982: Alain

So finally, *The Corn Mother* is going ahead.

I made all those arthouse films in the sixties and even some in the seventies. Heady times and a lot of fun. A lot of freedom. The last few years the quality of things I get to work on has been not so great. I've been over in America making some stuff I'm not even sure I wanted to have my name on. Dross really but entertaining in its own way.

Conrad and Gines invited me over. Somehow or other they set up a successful film production company over there. Made a lot of money. It's Gines' company really, he has the final say but he lets Conrad work on a passion project every now and again. I think he realises that it helps keep him quiet, keeps him towing the line. Plus he knows that Conrad draws in the talent. Some of them prefer to know that they're working with somebody with a critically revered background, rather than just someone who made tin cans and car tyres.

Gines has seen a couple of the more mainstream versions of the script. That's what he's given the green light for. I've still got one of the others stashed away and, I think, with Conrad's help, I might be able to, if not make that one, then at least bring some of the ideas from it into the film.

1982: Peter

Well, you'll never guess what? I got a phone call today from David who used to be my agent. He says that the script for *The Corn Mother* has sold. It's going into production later this year.

Blimey. I never thought that would happen. I'd not forgotten about it but I'd filed it away, under a heading of alternative lives. I'd been getting on with day-to-day life, being a good lad, coming to work, writing all this throwaway stuff for the paper and paying the bills. Mary had the baby, a bonny young lad we called Patrick and she's expecting again.

We got a council flat after Patrick arrived and we've set up home. Life's not too bad really.

I'm not sure how much I'll have to do with the production. From what David was saying I can just step back and wait for the cheque to arrive.

1982: Sarah

I have to say I'm enjoying working on this film. I saw some of the director Alain's earlier films back in my student days. They were the sort of films at that age you liked to be able to say you'd seen. You know, all arty and that.

Actually, though his films were arty, they were accessible to. Entertaining as well as being talking points. And although *The Corn Mother* is a bit trashy in parts, I can see that he's quietly trying to elevate it a little, add a few extra layers of meaning to it.

Some of the visuals remind me of those pop videos that are becoming ever more popular and I seem to have spent quite a bit of my time looking like an extra in a Kate Bush video. All ethereal and otherworldly as the villagers see me in their dreams and nightmares.

1982: Peter

Remember I said I wasn't going to have all that much to do with the production of the film? That's not quite what happened. It turns out that Alain was directing it, he got in touch with me, and the next thing I knew I was on set, making last minute changes to the script and tucking into the catering.

Mary wasn't happy of course. I had to take an unpaid sabbatical from work but... well, I just had to do it.

I'd never been on a filmset before. There was a lot of sitting around waiting for things to be set up, take after take of some shots. And then there's the British weather. Maybe setting a fair bit of the story in the country and outside wasn't such a good idea. We had a particularly wet September but I managed to work some of that into the revisions. Storm-drenched villagers cowering from the rain and their guilt. I think it worked pretty well.

I'm looking forward to seeing the finished thing. I've got a vision in my mind's eye of how its going to look but its hard to know for definite until you see it fully edited and finalised.

1982: Gines

That Alain. Thinks he's God's gift to filmmaking. Made a few arty films that crossed over and made a bit of money and he still thinks he's got it, still thinks he can do what he likes.

Well, this is my money he's playing with. My hard-earned cash. If he thinks he's sneaking all his highbrow ideas into the film he's wrong. I want paying punters for this one, for all of them actually, not just column inches in the broadsheets.

He's off the film. I'm telling him tonight. I know he'll kick up a fuss but what can he do? He's got the rights to nothing. They're all mine.

1982: Richard

I've been working on this film for far too long now. I'm not sure if it'll ever be finished. I don't know where the director is today, I'm not sure anybody does. It won't make all that much difference if he does turn up, the state he's likely to be in. It's the booze you see. And that's probably the least of it. Some people have a cup of tea and an egg on toast for breakfast. Not him. Not that I've ever seen. Breakfasts for him are a bit more likely to be purely liquid in form, and poured from a bottle that's lucky if it's survived from the day before.

I'm not all that high-up in the hierarchy of filmmaking, I never really have been and I'm not sure if I want to be. Yeh, I know, the higher up you go the more kudos you get, the more money. Also, though, the more politics and nonsense you have to deal with. The more likely it is that your ego will climb higher with you.

No, I'm not that important but without me, or all the unsung folk like me, your hour and a half or so of escape in the dream palace would be a blurry mess and the sound all over the place. And not in an arthouse manner. No, just a mess.

Which brings me back to this film. I'm not sure quite what it is that we're making. Some days I think it's more an intellectual arthouse piece, others it seems more like yet another of those films that are full of shock and horror, aimed directly at the shelves of the video rental shops that have sprung up across the land.

Those places are like stepping into an untamed frontier of culture. One that's busy not even testing boundaries but just doesn't even know that they exist. Nothing's legally certified and I don't know about you but at one of my local ones you're as likely to be given a bootleg copy when you rent a film as the official cassette.

1983: Ellen

It's not a bad job this one. The pay's okay and they're not scrimping on the soundtrack recording - I'm in a decent studio and I've been able to hire CS-80 and Prophet V synths. There's been some of the usual nonsense from a couple of the blokes in the studio, expecting me to make the tea but that settled down after a day or two when they realised I knew more than they did.

I think initially the plan had been to put a traditional instrument orientated soundtrack on the album, maybe something a bit folk-ish even but somebody in the production company had worked on pop promos and that'd given them a love of synth pop and electronic music, what with that being all over the charts at the moment. And so, here I am.

I'm thinking something a bit like John Carpenter and Alan Howarth's soundtrack for *Halloween III: Season of the Witch* might suit some of the sections. Something with an unsettled, tense atmosphere but still with plenty of melody.

1984: Ellen

Always get an advance. I know that now. I'd put in a lot of hours on that soundtrack, battling with temperamental synths, syncing it all to the onscreen action. I thought I'd done some of my best work and it was pretty much finished, we were just tinkering really while we waited for final approval from the production company.

I've not got a single note of it, only what I can play back in my head. I got into the studio one morning and all the tapes were gone, as were my reference notes and lists of settings. Nobody else who worked in the actual studios, the engineers or anybody, was there, so I asked the receptionist what was going on. They just shrugged, said something about problems with the production company.

I asked if they knew where the tapes had gone. More shrugs. The only thing they knew was that the hire companies were coming to collect the synths that afternoon.

1984: Peter

Well, what a fuck up.

I could just leave it there but I suppose I should say some more. The film had been edited and was, I think, ready to go. And then it all came out. Gines had not just his fingers in the till, more a shovel day and night. The receivers were called in and now the film's in limbo. Nobody seems to quite know who owns it or even where the finished reels are.

Half the cast and crew still haven't been paid, the other half have had something but everybody's on a promise that's never coming true.

And you can guess which half I'm part of. Mary's furious. She'd been looking forward to a holiday with me, the kids and her folks. A proper family do by the seaside but that's not happening any time soon now.

So I've been back at the paper for a while now. That bloody woman Thatcher got in again last year. Four more years of decimating those who aren't on the gravy train. Smashing. And now she's taken the miners on and they're getting a hiding. I've been reporting on it a bit but what makes it into the paper is skewed towards one side more than a little. And if you fancy having a go at some more guessing then I expect you can work out which side its leaning towards.

1984: Richard

I'd moved from technical assistance on the film to helping out with the edit and there was no way I was walking out of there without the reels. I reckon I got them all. Somebody had said recently that there'd already been a duplicate printing negative made but I'm not sure it actually happened.

I don't think anybody knows I took them. Maybe that night watchman. But I don't think he cares too much.

And so now I've got them at home. I've put them away down in the cellar, boxed up. Carol never really looks there and even if she does I expect she'll just think that it's more clutter from work. There's plenty of it elsewhere in the house.

I put in months on that film. Stayed loyal to it even after the money had started to dry up and they replaced the director with that lush. I'd heard somebody from the production company say that the film, the dailies and everything, all the footage, was probably going to be junked, which I couldn't let happen after all the hard work that had gone into it.

Maybe when all the noise and shouting about the finances has calmed down I'll let somebody know where they are.

Maybe.

1984: Gerry

It's been a funny old week. I work at a video duplication place and sometimes we make up smaller runs that are used as promotional tapes to send around the trade shows and magazines, the distributors and so on.

I'd made up this small batch of a film called *The Corn Mother*. Some kind of horror thing I think. It hadn't been shown at the cinema and was going straight to video.

I boxed them up and put them to one side, the plan was for them to be sent out the following day.

Anyways, I got in the next morning and they were nowhere to be seen. There was nothing in the collections book about them already having been picked up so I asked Reg the supervisor about it.

He got properly shifty. Looked worried as well. Said there'd been a cancellation on the order and not to worry about it. I asked him about the invoice as I didn't want to end up getting a roasting about them not being paid for. He just brushed it aside, said it had all been sorted but I looked and there's nothing in the files. It's odd as he's normally so by the book.

If he says it's sorted then I guess it is. It's not worth worrying about, especially as I've got a busy day making copies of some film called *The Keep*. I've watched a bit of the master copy to check the quality before I set the machines rolling. Seems like an odd film. Set in small rural village area, a bit horror, a bit supernatural. Reminded me in part of a pop video. Not all that different in a way to the bits of *The Corn Mother* that I saw when I was getting ready to duplicate that.

He needs to watch where he's going that Reg. He had a right shiner on one of his eyes. I asked him about it but he said he'd just dropped a box of tapes when he was getting it off the shelf. Strange that. I've never seen him lift anything heavier than a teacup or his pay packet.

1991: Peter

I was in the video rental shop the other day. They're more like respectable businesses nowadays. Less like slightly shady places with shelves full of all kinds of stuff from the X-rated sides of cinema.

There's even this American chain called Blockbuster that's been opening shops in the UK, with corporate branding and staff in uniforms.

I'd heard that back in the eighties there were some promotional copies made of *The Corn Mother* and there were plans to release it on video but it never seemed to happen and I don't even know if the original film reels still exist.

But even knowing that, I still half expect to see a copy of it when I'm in the rental shop, though I know I never will. It always makes me a bit wistful looking along the shelves.

I sort of lost touch with the film world after all that hassle with Gines and the subsequent fall out, and apart from when I'm in here I don't really think about back then all that much. I've got my job and my family and they both keep me pretty busy.

That young chap who ate baked beans while he toiled away at script revisions seems like another person to me now. Somebody I once met who told me about it, rather than it being me with ink on my fingers and a head full of ideas and dreams. Dreams of the corn mother and her nighttime kingdom.

1992: Sarah

You'll never guess what happened. My agent forwarded me a letter from somebody wanting to know if they could interview me about *The Corn Mother* for a fanzine they're planning.

I've not thought about that film for years. I just wanted to put it all behind me after it never came out and I didn't get properly paid.

I did get a bit of money from it but I had to sign a contract saying that I wouldn't talk about it in the press. I think that was the result of legal action by one of the producers to stop anybody involved from ruining his reputation. What was his name? Oh yes, Gines. From what I heard he dodged the bullet after being caught with very sticky fingers when his production company collapsed. Probably still managing to live the high life somewhere sunny I expect.

I'd quite like to talk about it, even if it's just for a fanzine. It's almost as though it never existed, like it was an imaginary film. But it's not worth the problems. Life's too short.

1993: Alain

There's to be a retrospective of my work at a prestigious film festival. Of course, they're concentrating on my earlier films rather than my more director for hire work that I've doing for the last decade or more now. Still, a retrospective's a retrospective.

I'd really love to show *The Corn Mother*. I know it's not all my work, that somebody else directed parts of it but from a rough cut I saw after I'd been replaced a fair bit of the spirit of what I was trying to do was still in the film and hopefully made it into the final edit. And it's never been seen. Never had a release, so it would be quite the story to show it.

I thought that maybe Gines would have mellowed about it all over the years. I tried contacting his people, even tried to phone him directly, see if anything could be done. I just came up against one brick wall after another. Eventually I resorted to flying over to his mansion hideaway. They wouldn't even open the gates for me. Gines wouldn't talk to me.

A month or so later I got a letter in the post. Inside was a copy of a paid invoice for the disposal of film materials. It was addressed to Gines' production company and the date was 1984. There was no note or other explanation with it. I can only think that it's Gines' way of telling me that the film doesn't exist anymore, that it was thrown out when everything imploded.

I phoned Conrad and he said he couldn't remember any film reels being disposed of but they might well have been, without his knowledge, as he didn't tend to have all that much to do with the day-to-day running of things, and even less so when the walls came crashing down. He said he'd just wanted out of there.

3/4

1994: Andrew

So, here I am at another film convention. Somebody had told me that he'd heard about this bloke who had a stall at it who said he had a copy of *The Corn Mother*.

Of course, it wasn't true. It was just yet another person who claimed to know somebody who'd seen it.

I can't tell you how much of my life I've spent thinking about and looking for this film. Ever since I was a kid in the mid-eighties and I heard the guy behind the counter and a customer talking about it in my local video rental shop. I'd been looking at the family film section, while sneaking glances over towards the zombie films, wandering if I could get away with renting *Poltergeist*. And all the time I was listening to what they were saying.

They'd talked about this mythical lost film called *The Corn Mother* that they wanted to see, about how a handful of promotional video copies were said to have been made and planned to be sent out to the trade before it was pulled from the rental release schedules and nobody in the industry had ever received a copy.

One of them said they'd heard it was nearer to the original director's earlier films, his more arthouse ones, while the other said from what he knew it was more like all the horror trash that littered the shelves of the shop. They talked about the different versions of the film's script they'd read, ordered from an obscure mail order company's advert in the back of a science fiction magazine, but they couldn't decide which was more likely to have gone into production.

It seemed to open something up in my mind and create a fascination with the lost worlds of this film, a dreamscape with this unknown treasure at the end of it.

2003: Andrew

I thought when the internet began to get big that something would turn up. But it didn't.

I can't tell you how many times I've searched for the phrase "The Corn Mother film" online. It's always the same old stories rolled out, the same often misinformed histories. I know all of it and more but still I'll read the articles, follow the discussions in forums and just search, search and search again.

I try not to talk to people I know about it too much. I've seen their glazed over expressions, their polite nods of interest (that stopped being quite so polite a while ago now). I don't really understand how this has gotten under my skin quite so much. From time to time I joke with myself about how I'm like one of King Arthur's Knights searching for the Holy Grail but my search seems infinitely more trivial. It's just a film I'm looking for. Not even one that anybody is sure is any good. But it's my Grail, my search and I seem to need to keep seeking it out, no matter how unlikely my succeeding is.

2006: Andrew

I came across this site which launched last year that hosts videos online. Anybody can upload more or less whatever they want and it seems fairly unregulated and to be turning a blind eye to copyright. People are posting music videos, daft recordings of their pets, shaky videos of nights out and gigs, well-known and obscure films and TV programmes broken up into sections. All of human life and culture really.

What do you think I've mainly been looking for? Yes, *that* film. And of course it's come back a big empty zero, apart from a few people mentioning it in comments below other videos.

2009: Andrew

Back in the late eighties and into the nineties I'd tried sending letters to people involved in the film, the cast, crew, production company and so on, asking them about it. Asking if they'd be prepared to be interviewed about *The Corn Mother*. I don't know what my aim was. I just wanted more definite proof that it had existed I suppose and I'd thought about putting together a fanzine about it.

That was another big empty zero. Mind you it was hard back then to find the addresses of film people and then to know if they read the letters that were sent to them. Often I'd just send them to, say, their agent's address and hope for the best.

To a degree the internet has changed that but less than you might think. Some industry people have their own website with a contact email or form but you never really know if they're picking up any message you send or if somebody else runs their site for them. Anybody of any stature generally has layer after layer of agents and so on to guard them from, well, random people like me who want to know about some obscure film that they worked on more than a quarter of a century ago.

And then there are the rumours. Rumours that nobody really wants to talk about the film after they weren't paid properly, that they'd rather just forget about it and even whispers that there are legal gagging orders in place to stop them discussing it.

Which of course is catnip to my quest. There's nothing like a good bit of unknowable and unprovable backstory myth around a film to help nurture its cult status.

2017: Andrew

Over the last five or six years I've noticed this phrase folk horror turning up more and more when I've searched for *The Corn Mother* online. It's a particular niche area of culture that focuses on a sense of the rural and folk culture as having an uncanny flipside. The film *The Wicker Man* seems to be a particular touchstone and recurring reference point for it all.

There are books, albums, social media groups, all kinds of things that are being called folk horror.

And given the subject matter of *The Corn Mother* it's not a huge surprise that is has started to be referenced in connection with folk horror. It's even on this huge list of folk horror-esque film and television that's been put together at one of the main online film websites. It's at number 37 in a list that runs to several hundred. Which surprises me as it seems impossible to see, so I suppose it's there more because of the intrigue that surrounds it, rather than as a comment on how good or relevant to folk horror the film is.

For years I'd half-hope each time I wandered into a video rental shop that I'd one day see *The Corn Mother* on its shelves but that's unlikely to happen now. I might find it somewhere but its unlikely to be a rental shop. The entire landscape of how people watch films has changed a lot over recent years. Video rental shops were once nearly as ubiquitous as corner shops but now they're nearly all gone, as people more and more watch stuff online. Even the big corporate chain Blockbuster shut its doors.

For a decade or two there were various mailorder rental DVD companies here and abroad but now there's just one of those left in the UK.

I suppose to a degree you could say video rental has been nationalised as some local council run libraries still rent them out but I think the days of that being the case are somewhat numbered.

2017: Andrew

I'm not so young anymore. Not yet old but definitely not young anymore. And this quest has taken up much of my life.

Well, that makes it sound like the central part of my life, which it isn't. I've had a conventional education and jobs (searching for obscure cult films doesn't put a lot of food on the table or coal in the fireplace, so needs must), a family, a broken heart, a broken marriage and all the rest.

But it's always stayed with me, this quest for this mythical film.

It has become a form of modern-day mythology for me. I suppose when you live in a more secular society you might still want to have your own versions of myths and fairy tales, the unknown, the other. This is my version of that.

The internet has fed the flames of that myth, with its never-ending spaces for discussion, sharing, commenting and voracious need for content. Stories with no end, like the "Will it, won't it be found?" of *The Corn Mother* are ideally suited to its open-ended nature.

I suppose you're thinking "But surely somebody would have spoken up by now? If the film existed and if maybe a few preview copies were made then surely something would have resurfaced?"

You'd think so wouldn't you?

The modern world leaves few spaces in which culture can be truly lost but this seems to be one time it is. From what the rumour mill says, all copies of the film, both dailies and the edited finished reels, were destroyed back in the eighties. Some say it was an oversight and that they were just thrown away during a storage clearout, others suggest they may have been deliberately destroyed and there is much debate about if that's the case, then who arranged it?

All I know at the moment is that it seems as lost as *The Were-wolf*, which was a 1913 silent short said to be the first werewolf movie, all prints of which are thought to have been destroyed in 1924 during a fire at Universal Studios. I'd probably have more chance finding that.

2018: Andrew

When I first started thinking about finding *The Corn Mother* in the eighties, like most people, I only had chance to see a film during the few weeks it was showing at the cinema. Maybe after saving up a bit of pocket money I might be able to rent it when it was finally released on video or if it went straight to rental. Generally I couldn't buy it, as back then official copies of films mostly cost silly money as they were often only made for the rental market.

If you were lucky a few years later it might be shown on TV. Seeing it then meant noticing it in the TV listings and, if it was on later at night, setting up the video recorder's timer and hoping it worked okay. There are a fair few films that I saw most of and then I'd set the timer wrong and it wouldn't record the last five minutes or so.

All that's changed nowadays. You can see almost everything with just a few clicks of your remote. Either by starting a subscription for a streaming service or paying for individual films online. And that's before I get to all the DVD and Blu-ray releases. Both official ones and those available on sites that sell copies of films and TV programmes that have never been officially released, often not great quality and sometimes originally taped from a TV broadcast. Plus there are all the unofficial uploads of films on public video streaming sites.

But of course *The Corn Mother*'s never appeared on any of them.

It's a strange thing but it could be said that the idea of films being lost is an obsolete idea but it's not really true. There are some films that are thought to have been genuinely lost and also there are a lot more that you know exist but for rights reasons etc, they're very hard to see. Like *Hippie Hippie Shake* based on the memoirs of Richard Neville, the editor of underground sixties satirical magazine *Oz*. There seem to have been a few preview screenings of that and then it was just caught in some release limbo.

2018: Andrew

I was doing one of my periodic searches for *The Corn Mother* on-line the other day. I don't do that so much anymore. Maybe my passion for the whole search has died down. Maybe I'm just getting older and I'm starting to finally accept that I'm never going to see it.

In the search results there pops up this album called *The Corn Mother*. It's described as being "Reflections on an imaginary film" and the explanatory text that accompanies it is pretty much a potted history of the film's plot, it's production, non-release and all the rumours about people having seen it.

It's not accurate in all the details but not far off.

Strange that they've called it an imaginary film. Yes, it's near-mythical but it's not an imaginary film.

The album is said to be "an exploration of the whispers that tumble forth from the corn mother's kingdom, whisperings that have seemed to gain a life of their own".

I've ordered a copy. I'm looking forward to hearing it, seeing if it captures the spirit of the film that's been playing in my head for all these years.

2019: Andrew

Like happens with a lot of cultural movements, folk horror as a genre seems to have reached some kind of possibly saturated peak. I keep seeing it mentioned in mainstream national papers, book festival programmes, new films being called folk horror and so on.

Curiously though, *The Corn Mother* and the whole mystery around it doesn't seem to have caught the attention of mainstream pundits. You'd think it would be tailor made for at least one "lost film" article.

Maybe there have been some written but I've just missed them.

And although I'm more resigned to never finding it, there are some things that still keep me holding out hope that one day the film will turn up.

Like the long thought lost original psychedelic ending to Saul Bass' far from conventional take on the science fiction genre *Phase IV* being found. That was made in 1974 but the original ending wasn't discovered until 2012.

Initially after it was found it only got, I think, a brief showing at one cinema in the States but it's been released to stream at home now.

So you never know.

2020: Andrew

I looked today and *The Corn Mother* isn't on that online folk horror film list any more. Maybe they decided to take it off until somebody's actually seen it.

It's peculiar though, as I've also noticed the chatter about the film online is quietening down. It's falling off forum discussion groups. I'm not sure why. Perhaps these things just go in cycles.

2020: Andrew

I went to a film convention recently. You know how people who starred in cult films and television dramas over the last few decades can have a further stage in their careers, after the acting jobs have dried up, by appearing and doing paid for signings at conventions? Well, somebody who was in *The Corn Mother* was at one of them.

(Actually, even still quite active and famous actors have been appearing at them for a while now, what with science fiction, fantasy and superhero genres having become such big business.)

As far as I know it had never happened before that somebody from *The Corn Mother* had made an appearance at a convention. A bit unusual that, as you would've thought somebody would have done, even if it was just one of the people with a cameo part.

Although it was quite a trek to get there I still went. I was going to ask them about the film. Face to face.

They were doing a signing and I paid my money and queued up. When my turn came they asked me who I'd like the signature made out to. It was now or never.

I asked them if they had any particular memories of *The Corn Mother*. They just looked blank. Not annoyed. Not like they didn't want to talk about it. Just blank. They asked me if I was sure I'd got the name of the film right, as they couldn't remember that one.

I said yes I was sure but I got the same blank response and so I mumbled something and stepped away. I know they've been in a lot of stuff, worked on over a hundreds films and television programmes, and it's heading towards 30 years ago that it was made, and they had a relatively small part in it, so maybe they'd just forgotten about it.

2021: Andrew

I know it was made. I've read about it. It's been written about a fair old bit. I've had conversations about it. Asked at conventions if anybody had a copy and they didn't say "Never heard of it", they'd just say something like they were looking for it as well.

But last week when I looked it up online I couldn't find any mention apart from that album I bought and some references to corn mother folklore. There's not another single word anywhere about it.

I thought maybe it was just a blip online. Some search engine algorithm had gone out of sync, servers gone down or something. A whole pile of coincidences that had happened at once.

I've searched again every day since. It's still not there. There's nothing at archive.org that stores a lot of old web pages either. I asked and emailed people I know about it and I just got a similar blank response as that actor gave me at the film convention last year.

But I've got the notes I made all those years ago for the fanzine up in the loft somewhere, my printouts of internet pages, the magazines where it's mentioned. They're all here. All of them.

2022: Jack

This lady asked me to come and clear out her husband's stuff. I wasn't sure if he'd passed away or they'd split up and he'd left it all behind, and I didn't want to ask and upset her. You just have to get on with the job in that situation.

There were plenty of old cameras and lenses, some dark-room equipment. I'm not sure if anybody really wants that stuff anymore. Maybe a few collectors online buy that kind of thing. Valerie would know more about that.

Down in the cellar there was more of the same and a few boxes with film reels in them. I asked her about those. She didn't seem to know a lot about them, said he used to bring home all kinds of stuff from work, hated seeing things thrown away.

It's not really my line. Old furniture and nick-nacks, that's what I tend to look out for. What I know about.

2022: Valerie

Jack came back from a house clearance today. Mostly old junk and things destined for the skip. A few nice old cameras. I told him how they get used as ornaments nowadays and some people have even started using them again, so they're worth putting out in the shop. He just looked at me gone out, said something about couldn't they just use their phone and did Boots even develop films anymore.

One thing that caught my eye was these boxes with film reels in them. You know those old fashioned looking silver canisters that take you back to another era. The kind of things cinemas used. A fair few of those. I asked Jack about them but he said the woman whose house they were from didn't seem to know all that much about them.

Most of the canisters were unmarked but one had, I think, *The Corn Mother* written on it. It was faded and scuffed, so it was hard to be sure. I don't know if this kind of thing goes for much or if you're even allowed to sell them if they were used in cinemas. I'll have to look it up online.

2022: Valerie

So, I looked up online for any details of a film called *The Corn Mother*, to see if there'd been any sales of related memorabilia and the like. There was nothing on any of the auction house's sites in previous sales or on that main public auction site that I use from time to time.

In fact I could only find a handful of mentions of a film with that name; they were all about this album soundtrack for it, which talked about it being an "imaginary film", which I'd say isn't quite true, as, if it were, well, what's cluttering up my stockroom?

Actually, that's not quite right. There was one other mention. On some film fans forum. Somebody called Andrew589 asking for any information about *The Corn Mother* film.

I might send him a message tomorrow when the shop quietens down a bit.

Scene fades to black.
Credits roll.

About

The Corn Mother novella is a further exploration of an imaginary near-mythical film which first began on an album released with the same name in 2018, which featured music by a number of different performers.

The world, stories and dreamscapes of *The Corn Mother* are also explored on the album *The Corn Mother: Night Wraiths*, which was released simultaneously with the novella in 2020. That album was written and recorded by Stephen Prince, the novella's author, and is both a soundtrack to accompany it and a standalone piece of work set amongst "the whispers that tumble forth from the corn mother's kingdom".

All three have been released as part of the *A Year In The Country* project, which is a set of year-long explorations of otherly pastoralism and the undercurrents and flipsides of bucolic dreams; a wandering amongst work that draws from the further reaches of folk culture, the hidden and underlying tales of the land and where they meet and intertwine with the spectral histories, lost futures and parallel worlds of hauntology. As a project, it has included a website featuring writing, artwork and music which stems from that otherly pastoral/spectral hauntological intertwining, alongside a growing catalogue of album and book releases.

The *A Year In The Country* non-fiction books and written posts on the website are intended to draw together and connect layered and, at times, semi-hidden cultural pathways and signposts, journeying from acid folk to edgelands via electronic music innovators and pioneers and folkloric film and photography.

The project was created in 2014 by Stephen Prince and the roots of its inspiration can be found in part amongst a childhood spent in the shadow of the Cold War, discovering the fringes of science fiction and related dystopian tales at an age when he was probably too young to fully understand them, while also living amongst and next to the British countryside and overlooked edgelands.

Further details about *A Year In The Country* can be found at its main website: www.ayearinthecountry.co.uk

Notes on the Book's Structure

The book's structure is inspired by the cycle of the year. Following the number of seasons, it is split into four sections; it has 52 chapters (which could also be considered scenes or episodes), the same number as there are weeks in the year; relating to the number of days in a non-leap year, each chapter's text contains no more than 365 words.

Thanks to:

Those who contributed music to *The Corn Mother* album released in 2018, as well as other *A Year In The Country* released albums: Gavino Morretti, Pulselovers, The Heartwood Institute, United Bible Studies, Depatterning, Widow's Weeds, Sproatly Smith and Field Lines Cartographer. Also Ian Lowey for *The Corn Mother* album's design and layout, alongside his other dab hand design and editorial work for *A Year In The Country*.

The other performers who have contributed music to the *A Year In The Country* releases: including Grey Frequency, Hand of Stabs, Michael Tanner, David Colohan, The Straw Bear Band, Polypores, The Rowan Amber Mill, Spaceship, Time Attendant, Cosmic Neighbourhood, Circle/Temple, Keith Seatman, Kitchen Cynics, Listening Center, Alaska, Panabrite, Unknown Heretic, Phonofiction, Magpahi, Lutine, Vic Mars, Bare Bones, Endurance, Sharron Kraus, Dom Cooper, Quaker's Stang, Embertides, Howlround, The Hare And The Moon, Racker & Orphan, The British Space Group, Unit One, Sophie Cooper, Harriet Lisa, Neil Whitehead, Dave Millsop, Zosia Sztykowski, The Soulless Party, She Rocola, Assembled Minds, Handspan, Folclore Impressionista and The Séance.

The people who have sold the *A Year In The Country* releases and/or lent their advice; Jim Jupp of Ghost Box Records, The state51 Conspiracy in particular Shaun Yule, Juno Records, Piccadilly Records, Psilowave, Centre de Cultura Contemporánia de Barcelona, all at Norman records especially Ant and Phil and Justin Watson of Front & Follow.

All who have bought and supported the *A Year In The Country* music releases, books and artifacts and everybody that visits the website and/or shares etc posts elsewhere online.

Everybody who has written about *A Year In The Country* and reviewed the various releases, including John Coulthart, Simon

Reynolds, DJ Food, Jude Rogers, Ben Graham, Ian White, Matthew Sedition, Grey Malkin, Bob Fischer, Massimo Ricci, Warren Ellis, Sukhdev Sandhu, Joe Banks, Alan Boon and Dave Thompson and all at *Terrascope*, *Avant Music News*, *Music Won't Save You*, *Rockerilla*, *Starburst*, *Fortean Times*, *Bliss Aquamarine*, *Was Ist Das?*, *Shindig!*, *The Wire*, *The Active Listener*, *Include Me Out*, *Wyrd Daze*, *Folk Words*, *Landscapism*, *fRoots*, *The Sunday Experience*, *The Golden Apples of the Sun*, *Electronic Sound*, *Both Bars On*, *Rue Morgue*, *Mojo*, *Folk Radio*, *Goldmine*, *Heathen Harvest*, *Saint Etienne Disco*, *Diabolique*, *Bandcamp Daily*, *Quiet World & Wonderful Wooden Reasons*, *Incendiary*, *Violet Apple*, *33-45*, *Radio Limbo*, *We Are Cult*, *Folk Horror Revival*, *Forestpunk*, *Whisperin' & Hollerin'*, *A Closer Listen*, *Mind De-Coder*, *The Guardian*, *Moof* and *Psychogeographic Review*.

All those who have included *A Year In The Country* released tracks in their radio broadcasts, podcasts etc, including Stuart Maconie, Gideon Coe, Chris Lambert, Nick Luscombe and all at *Evening of Light*, *Kites and Pylons*, *More Than Human*, *The OST Show*, *Syndae*, *Sunrise Ocean Bender*, *Fractal Meat*, *Flatland Frequencies*, *The Unquiet Meadow*, *Gated Canal Community Radio*, *Phantom Circuit*, *Free Form Freakout*, *The Séance*, *The Crooked Button*, *Project Moonbase*, *Awkward Moments*, *Pull the Plug*, *Pic n' Mix*, *On the Wire* and *You, the Night & the Music*.

Verity Sharp for inviting me onto *Late Junction* and Rebecca Gaskell for her admirable production of the show, Suzy Prince for the proofing and editing, Gary Milne of BBC Archives for his compiling and curation of video spectres, William "Billy" Harron as always for accidentally pointing me in the direction of the undercurrents of folk, my family for the ongoing support and to everybody whose work has inspired me on the wanderings through the explorations and pathways of *A Year In The Country*.

Thanks and a tip of the hat to you all!